# Golden Gate Bridge

Lori Dittmer

Creative Education · Creative Paperbacks

# Road map of Contents

# San Francisco
## California

**W**elcome to the Golden Gate Bridge! This **suspension bridge** connects San Francisco and Marin counties in California. It is one of the longest bridges of its kind in the United States!

The Golden Gate **Strait** flows under the bridge. This is where the San Francisco Bay meets the Pacific Ocean. The bridge was named for this place.

# How long is the

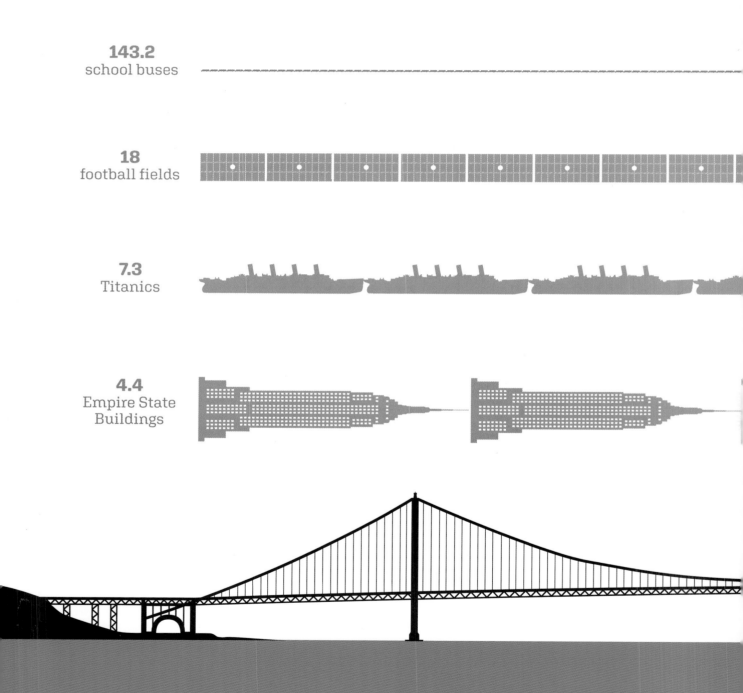

**143.2**
school buses

**18**
football fields

**7.3**
Titanics

**4.4**
Empire State
Buildings

# Golden Gate Bridge?

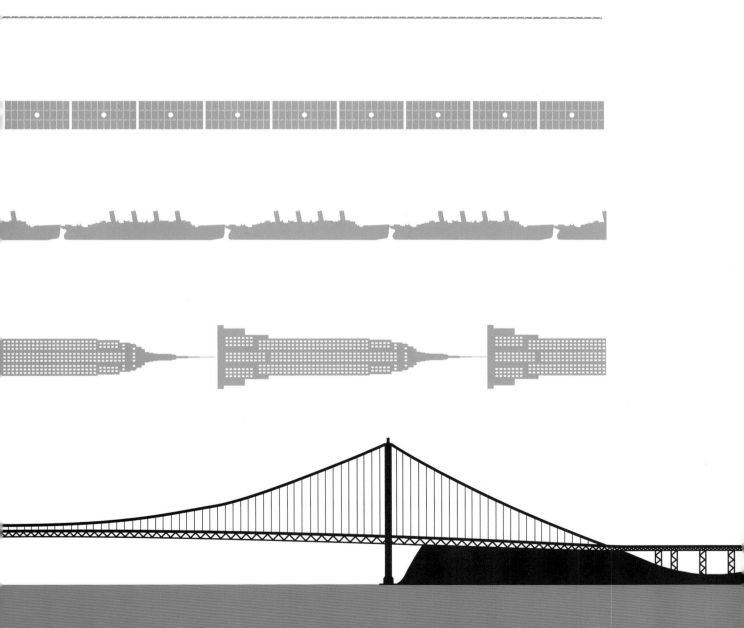

**D**uring the 1800s, boating was the only way across the strait. Some people wanted a bridge built. Others worried it would not be safe. Earthquakes frequently rumble there. Strong winds whip the area.

**B**y the 1930s, many people drove cars. City leaders thought a bridge would help San Francisco grow. Joseph Strauss led the project. Work started in 1933, during the **Great Depression**. People who needed jobs came to work on the bridge.

Golden Gate Bridge
◀ under construction ▶

Two metal towers support the bridge. One was built in deep water. More than 600,000 **rivets** hold each tower together. Thick steel cables support the weight of the bridge. The flexible bridge can sway. This has helped it remain standing in strong winds and earthquakes.

The Golden Gate Bridge opened in 1937. Vehicles cross the 1.7-mile (2.7 km) bridge in six lanes of traffic. Its orange color is easy for boats to see. Today, people constantly work on the bridge to keep it safe.

**B**illions of vehicles have crossed the bridge since it opened. You can also walk across on the sidewalk. Outdoor exhibits show how the bridge was built.

**Can you spot these in the picture above?**

**Palace of Fine Arts**

**Alcatraz Island**

**Fort Point**

**N**ext, stroll over to Fort Point. Learn about its history while enjoying the view of the bridge. Then explore the Golden Gate National Recreation Area.

# Build a Straw Suspension Bridge

-------------------- materials --------------------

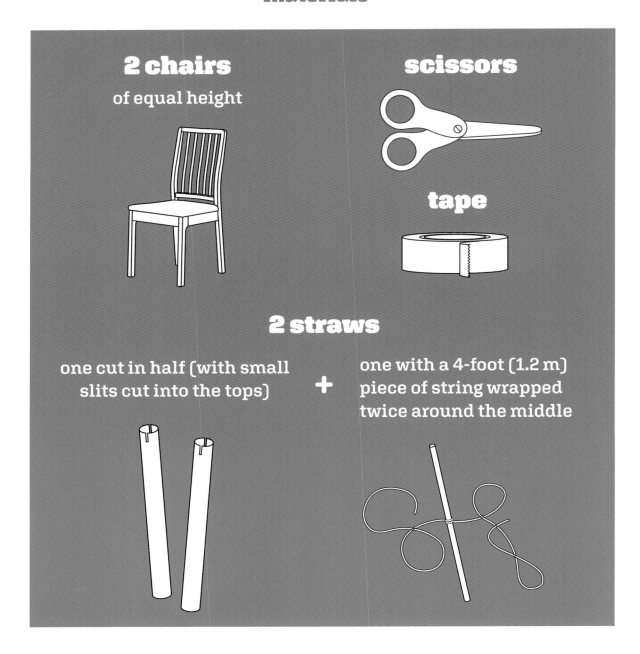

**2 chairs**
of equal height

**scissors**

**tape**

**2 straws**

one cut in half (with small slits cut into the tops)

**+**

one with a 4-foot (1.2 m) piece of string wrapped twice around the middle

**1**

Place the chairs seven inches (17.8 cm) apart, with seats facing each other.

7 inches

**2**

Tape one half of the cut straw to the outer edge of one of the chair seats. The slit should be on top. Tape the other straw half to the other chair in the same way.

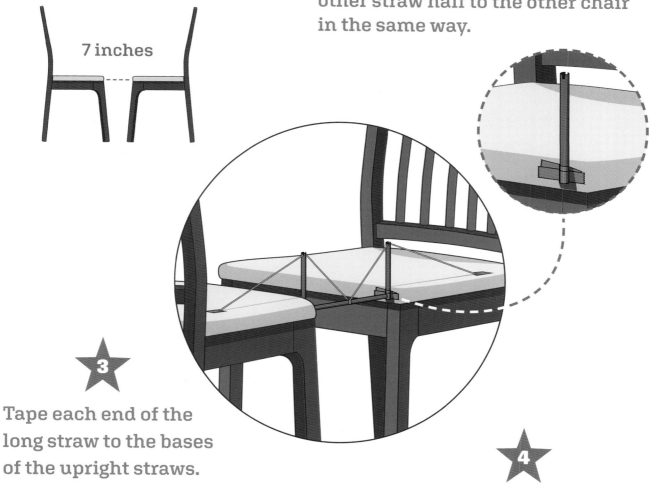

**3**

Tape each end of the long straw to the bases of the upright straws.

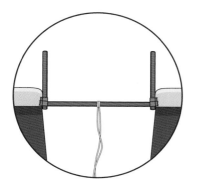

**4**

Thread the string through the slits on top. Then tape the rest of the string to each chair so that the "cable" is tight.

# Glossary

### ★ Great Depression ★

a time (1929–39) when the country's economy was in decline and many people lost their jobs and savings

### ★ rivets ★

short metal bolts that hold together pieces of metal

### ★ strait ★

a narrow passage of water connecting two large bodies of water

### ★ suspension bridge ★

a bridge in which the weight of the deck is supported by vertical cables hanging from larger cables that run between towers and are anchored at each end

# Read More

Finger, Brad. *13 Bridges Children Should Know*. New York: Prestel, 2015.

Reusser, Kayleen. *The Golden Gate Bridge*. Kennett Square, Penn.: Purple Toad, 2018.

# Websites

**YouTube: The Golden Gate Bridge for Kids: Famous Landmarks for Children**
Watch this video to learn more about the Golden Gate Bridge.

*https://www.youtube.com/watch?v=WKphjf3VZhA*

**YouTube: What Makes Bridges So Strong?**
Learn about how different bridges work.

*https://www.youtube.com/watch?v=oVOnRPefcno*

Note: Every effort has been made to ensure that the websites listed above are suitable for children, that they have educational value, and that they contain no inappropriate material. However, because of the nature of the Internet, it is impossible to guarantee that these sites will remain active indefinitely or that their contents will not be altered.

# Index

**PUBLISHED BY CREATIVE EDUCATION
AND CREATIVE PAPERBACKS**
P.O. Box 227, Mankato, Minnesota 56002
Creative Education and Creative Paperbacks
are imprints of The Creative Company
www.thecreativecompany.us

**LIBRARY OF CONGRESS CATALOGING-
IN-PUBLICATION DATA**
Names: Dittmer, Lori, author.
Title: Golden Gate Bridge / Lori Dittmer.
Series: Landmarks of America.
Includes bibliographical references and index.
Summary: Examining the building process
from the ground up, this high-interest title
covers the history and construction of the
Golden Gate Bridge, one of California's most
well-known landmarks.

Identifiers: LCCN: 2018061066
ISBN 978-1-64026-125-9 (hardcover)
ISBN 978-1-62832-688-8 (pbk)
ISBN 978-1-64000-243-2 (eBook)

Subjects: LCSH: Golden Gate Bridge (San
Francisco, Calif.)—Juvenile literature.
/ Suspension bridges—California—San
Francisco—Juvenile literature.
Classification: LCC TG25.S225 D58 2019
DDC 624.2/309794/61—dc23

**DESIGN AND PRODUCTION**
by Joe Kahnke; art direction by Rita Marshall
Printed in China

**PHOTOGRAPHS** by Alamy (Della Huff),
Getty Images (Al Greene Archive/Frederic
Lewis/Archive Photos, John Elk/Lonely
Planet Images, ferrantraite/E+, Roger
Ressmeyer/Corbis/VCG, Underwood
Archives/Archive Photos), iStockphoto
(bluejayphoto, photoquest7, VladSt),
Shutterstock (BATKA, John Bilous,
bmphotographer, dikobraziy, f11photo, Jody,
Ranier Lesniewski, Nickolay Stanev)

**FIRST EDITION** HC 9 8 7 6 5 4 3 2 1
**FIRST EDITION** PBK 9 8 7 6 5 4 3 2 1